MA·NIP·U·LA·TION:

The action of manipulating someone in a clever or unscrupulous way.

Sometimes situations arise that are out of our control. We reach for the hands of others and trust that they can guide us, help us, and *heal us.* Truth is, sometimes these people hurt us more than we ever expected. Sometimes the people we encounter in life are nothing but a lesson. And the lesson in this all is to be self-aware. Understand your fears, your triggers, your emotions both good and bad and spend time with yourself. Fall in love with yourself the way you desperately want others to. The only mistake you make in life is giving someone else power over you. You are stronger than your pain...

I am stronger than my pain.

LOVE 9

Daddy's Girl 10

Haunted 16

Broken 18

I'm Okay 21

9-1-1 23
My Thorne 28

Closure 32

Her First Love 36

I Do 39

My Guardian Angel 41

SEX 47

Inside 48

Scarlett Letter 50

Guys Like You 53

Master of Manipulation 54

Fuck Him 58

After Hours 63

*Blackout 68

DEPRESSION 73

First Date Questions 74

Replaced 76

Caged Thoughts 79

Homesick 82

Monkey Bars of Hope 84

3:28AM 86

Too Late 89

*To Everyone I've Ever Loved 92

***TRIGGER WARNING**

LOVE.

"Daddy's Girl."

The first man in my life seemed to be nonexistent

Physically he was there but emotionally he was distant

So, every night I stayed awake praying to God wishing

That one day we could have a bond like the one that we were missing

It was easy to fall behind, always being in the middle

"Pain heals within time" and yet I still remain crippled

Long nights where I called for him, and he was nowhere to be found

Walking in and out emotionally, like a door spinning round

He worked hard, and sacrificed so much for me

I would've known him all my life, but that choice wasn't up to me

See, 'cause, he worked late most days, and days off he spent worn out

His silence broke my brick walled heart, I let him break me down

I wrote a poem about him when I was just about 12 years old

I knew I had a gift in me, just never thought I'd be so bold

The prompt said to write "where you're from, or wish to be"

So, I wrote "I'm from a place where you never seem to be"

In and out of therapy, for over 10 years straight

But you never believed in my disease you said it was always fake

I couldn't trust a professional, because I couldn't have trusted you

It's worse now 'cause I don't know love, 'cause I never had it from you

You find partners like your parents

Pick and choose them then compare them

Then you say he's nothing like your dad, but he's as clear as he's transparent

He's straightforward and he's honest

Says he lies and breaks his promise

But you put him above everyone so he can win your contest

'Cause, love is something strange, it's foreign and it's new

And maybe I'd be less scared of change if you loved me like I loved you

I wanted you to protect me from the scary monsters under my bed

But as I grew older the monsters moved and made their way into my head

I needed you, but you never did come to my rescue

You never wanted to be there for me no matter how much I begged you

You didn't teach me how to love, I had to learn that the hard way

Life's a race here goes the guns and I never got to the start place

You didn't warn me about men, or teach me how to fight

We were under the same roof, but we lived a separate life

You were strict, and you were stern

'To live is the best way learned'

You taught me if I play with fire, I will end up burned

You didn't tell me why or how that fire was always steaming

You taught me the right answers, yeah, but not the correct meanings

So, I walk through life, questioning everyone else's intentions

I mirror back what I get but all I see is your reflection

And, I'm broken

. . . .

Who knows, maybe it's 'cause you are too

Still coping from the fact that your father left you

But because you didn't leave physically

You think it's not killing me

That you and I can't be in the same room for too long acting civilly

Do you even know why I'm always hurting?

Why I spend every weekend working?

It's 'cause I can't stand the thought of us talking face-to-face in person

'Cause, your idea of bonding is you on the couch downing bottles

Then you question why I'm so fucked up as if you were the perfect model

You criticize and you judge, you can't accept me for who I love

You always have the final say and what's been said is what's been done

And, I don't know how much longer I can sit back and remain silent

I always think about telling you how I feel but it's never the right time and

I lose my train of thought and all the words I glued together

'Cause when you look me in the eyes, I choke under all the pressure

And it's the same shit I go through with every single one of my partners

Guns blazing, hearts breaking 'cause I'm fighting without armor

It's that thick skin, that I have

Hurt people hurt people back

And I never knew how important it is for a daughter to be loved by her dad

Daddy issues...

Who would've thought it?

You had love for me before I just wonder when you lost it

Lost it,

All the respect for myself I lost it

There's a thin line between my heart and legs and every boy I meet they cross it

And I blame you

Because everywhere I turn, I search for acceptance

I search for trust, honesty, and dependence

I keep making mistakes and I never learn my lesson

So, when someone good comes around, I just keep on second guessing

'Cause, the only love I've known was the love I had to fight for

The kind of love you cried out in your bed and stayed up all night for

The kind of love that hurts if you let it get too close

The kind of love where ignoring meant, "I love you, the most"

And boy, did they love me...

At least, that's what I imagined

How else do you justify their negative words and actions?

My father, my partners, it's all a sick twisted cycle

Of does he love me, does he not, and I can't seem to shake this denial

I wish that you loved me, and I wish that you knew me

Not because I want a bond like the one they show in movies

Not because my outside doesn't match my inner beauty

Not because you feel like using the word "love" really loosely

Not because as a father it's your responsibility and duty

Not because if I die, you're afraid things will get spooky and your lack of love will always haunt you

I want you to love me for me, but more importantly because you want to.

"Haunted."

I deleted your number for the 10th time in a row

I don't see how it would help 'cause like the back of my hand it's something I'll always know

But I needed to be free,

Free from all the pain, all the hurt, I've had enough

Of giving you my heart when you don't even deserve my love

And I loved you, hard

You said "I got you when you fall" but why do I have all these scars

That you never bothered to fix, heal, or repair

Then you expect me to bend over backwards for you without clearing the air

You only text me when I'm seconds away from being done with you completely

I'd block your number but unlike you, I meant it when I said "I'm here if you need me"

So, what do you need?

'Cause it ain't me, and it sure as hell ain't sex

What happened? Did you see everyone walk out when you had nothing and realize I was the only one left?

'Cause when you love someone, that shit just doesn't fade

And when you hurt someone, that pain will always stay

So please, what do you want from me?

I finally stopped dreaming about you, so why do you keep haunting me?

And you do that shit on purpose, 'cause you know how fast I fall for you

Not taking into consideration the feelings of the people I hurt 'cause you know I'd risk it all for you

But, I can't keep doing that

'Cause when I think about it, the shit I do for you, you wouldn't do it back

So, where does that leave us?

Because I don't have enough holy water to fight off your demons

So please,

Can I continue to mourn the death of our relationship in peace?

"Broken."

Do you know what it was like pulling off to the side of the street?

Because I felt my chest collapsing and I swore I couldn't breathe

And the tears kept coming, making it harder and harder to see

Where I stood up late in my bed for almost six weeks

Because when I finally fell asleep you were in every one of my dreams

I didn't speak, I didn't eat

I couldn't move a muscle without my body feeling weak

I felt like I was dying

I screamed your name into my trembling hands, and wished you'd come back too

But I knew you had a past, and hey, I had a past too

But I never would've gone back and thrown away the future I had with you

You made promises to me, and we set goals to achieve

And now I'm watching you and her do all the things we said we'd be

Remember when we were close friends?

When you told me you loved me, and all the time that we spent

I look back at that all but I just can't pretend

That you didn't give me everything I ever hoped for just to let it all end

When you came into my life, a broken heart never occurred to me

Because you were the last person I thought of when I thought of who would hurt me

I never want to admit it,

But congratulations, you're the one who did it

The one who left me cut and all open

The one who left me destroyed and broken

Do you know what it was like pulling off to the side of the street?

Because I felt my chest collapsing and I swore I couldn't breathe

And the tears kept coming, making it harder and harder to see

Where I stood up late in my bed for almost six weeks

Because when I finally fell asleep you were in every one of my dreams

I didn't speak, I didn't eat

I couldn't move a muscle without my body feeling weak

And don't get me started with the permanent tears on my cheeks

I finally stopped crying, but you can still see the streaks

And the mascara on my pillowcase is a reminder everyday

Of how I never should've given you everything I had in the first place

I gave you my strength, my heart, my soul

I gave you my love and the remaining trust in me

I gave you so much I don't know what it's like to feel whole

And I never would've given you so much if I knew what it would've done to me.

"I'm Okay."

You left me, and that's okay

Because the memories will forever stay

You hurt me, and that's okay

Because your happiness means more to me than mine does anyway

You met someone, and that's okay

You love her now, and that's okay

You're smiling so much brighter every single day

You shine so bright even through the hardest of rain

And so long as you're happy I could care less about my pain

When you really love someone, I guess that's the price you gotta pay

And you know what? That's okay

Because the tears will stop falling one day

And even if they don't, I'll still be okay

It's all okay because I trusted you

I fell in love with you

You were the one person I admired, I looked up to you

But you led me to believe

That it was only me

Then strung her along the same time you were fucking me

You lied, you cheated

You made promises to me that you could never keep

You ripped

You shattered

You *destroyed* every part of me

Every part I had left, I gave you so effortlessly

I didn't want to trust you

And I didn't want to love you

If I knew right now that it wouldn't be enough for you

You broke everything, all that's left is the pain

All the pieces of me gone

And that's **not** okay.

"9-1-1."

"9-1-1, what's your emergency?"

It started off calm

Like nothing could go wrong

But like all relationships that 'honeymoon phase' don't last long

He bought my love through jewelry and flowers

And there wasn't a love story that compared to ours

He put me on a pedestal, and treated me like royalty

Never did I have to question his morale or loyalty

He held me down, when I needed it most

And I know nobody's perfect, but I swear he came so close

He extended his arms wide whenever I needed his guidance

And always knew what to say even if the answer was silence

It was perfect for months, so I never did expect it

To all go down south and things to get so hectic

It was your typical fights at first

***He* yelled, I cried, and things magically seemed to work**

Then somewhere along the lines I started my heavy drinking

And acted out on feelings when I wasn't clearly thinking

It was your typical fights at first

I yelled, *he* cried, and things magically seemed to work

Then somewhere along the lines, yelling just wasn't doing it

But I swore I loved him I just had a hard time proving it

I kept apologizing after every hurtful slur

But my apologies meant nothing when the whole night was a blur

Apologizing for events I don't recall occurred

It's absurd,

Looking back on my behavior

Screaming so loud that it woke up the neighbors

Accusing him of cheating with no trail on paper

I put my fist, to his deep dimpled cheeks

And the swelling didn't go down until a couple of weeks

He forgave me, and then the cycle repeats

It was your typical fights at first

I *hit*, he forgave, and things magically seemed to work

But somewhere along the lines, these fights grew more intense

Had to *beg* for his forgiveness 'cause this wasn't the first offense

So, earlier today I went out with some of my friends

And started drinking as if the day had no end

But something told me to rush back to his home

Because in the back of my mind, I swore he wasn't alone

I WAS BANGING ON THE DOOR, LIKE I WAS THE POLICE

AND EVERY SECOND THAT WENT BY MY ANGER INCREASED

THERE WAS NO NEED FOR EXPLAINING

'CAUSE I WAS WAY PAST COMMUNICATING

MY ANGER KEPT ESCALATING

AND HE HIT ME...

No hesitation

I fell to the ground, onto a chair, fan, and some cables

And maybe I wouldn't have fallen if I wasn't so unstable

I remember laying on the ground, shocked in disbelief

But, it's okay, because I hit him, so he hit me

But I knew I wasn't safe and that I had to leave

Because there was no stopping him, no matter how much I begged him to please

As I rushed to his room to grab my belongings

He put his hand over my mouth to prevent me from calling

I'm screaming like it's not 4 o'clock in the morning

I just wanted to go home, but I knew I wasn't sober

So, he grabbed my keys until my drunken rant was over

I started to walk out, and he followed close behind

I said "I had to go" and he hit me and said "**FINE!**"

And it's crazy…cause when you're drunk, there's some things you can't recall

But thank God for the blood that was smeared on the walls

I ran outside, hoping anyone could hear me

I waved down to the police but they didn't see me

And the neighbors, get this, wouldn't let *him* anywhere near me

But if only they knew the truth then they too, would fear me

I saw blood gush from my hand, down my leg and onto the street

How could I let this cycle repeat?

And the very next day, I spent in the hospital getting x-rays

Answering the questions they had on the survey

Because I had bruises on *my* wrists,

Bruises on *my* lips

Bruises on *my* arms, back, chest, knees, and hips

It started off calm

How did this go wrong?

Were the signs clearly there and we ignored them all along?

It was your typical fights at first

But after that night, nothing's ever seemed to work

I guess somewhere along the lines he realized this was too intense

I guess somewhere along the lines he found his inner strength

But I don't blame him, because it was self-defense

Because if the roles were reversed, well then, that would make sense.

"My Thorne."

Your smile seems bright

As your eyes fill with light

In a different way from when *I* was still in your life

Your presence is glowing

And your happiness is showing

Its way throughout your body and you don't even know it

Your mood has changed

The way you talk ain't the same

I guess walking out your life is the reason to blame

I guess walking out your life was a blessing to you

Because ever since I left, nothing is upsetting you

So, I don't know why I'm here confessing to you...

There's no doubt in my heart

The feelings I felt were strong from the start

And have only gotten stronger with this time apart

I miss you, I do

But we're opposites, me and you

It was a really great thing at first then it turned bad too

Many fights with our fists and guns blazing

After the nights that were so amazing

But neither of us knew what we were truly facing

A lifetime of hate, jealousy, and rage

Trapped with each other like an animal in a cage

How can we be together when we're not on the same page?

I want your happiness to outshine the sun

But I have failed you all these years, so I think my time is done

We're better off parting ways in the long run

All I ever wanted was someone like you...

Not *someone* like you,

All I ever wanted *was* you

Yet, I failed and failed you too many times before

So, this cuts me deep, deep down to the core

When I say I can't be with you anymore

I didn't want to speak those words into existence

Because I never thought breaking up would've existed

And now all you are to me is a memory in the distance

And every day I wake up praying and wishing

That we can just live in the moment so I can stop reminiscing

I miss it...

The late-night calls and random texts

The fights, your hugs, and makeup sex

The "I love you's" were always the best

Memories like yours I will never forget

But your heart was too strong, and I was too weak

I made promises to you I knew I couldn't keep

So now I sit back and wallow in my own grief

Thinking about all the goals we set to achieve

Are now the ones that are incomplete

Your love was different, than the others

The kind of love you hope to discover

That makes the dead of winter feel like the beginning of summer

The kind of love that makes you think "is this even real?"

The type of emotions you never thought you'd feel

From wounds and scars you **never** thought would heal

But everything does, and it feels so right

The happiest you've been so far in your life

Makes every battle worth every fight

But, with fighting comes tears

And all of my fears

That we won't make it in the next couple of years

So, how do we part, and say goodbye nicely

When the words I'm saying aren't being put lightly

The chances of us fixing things is highly unlikely

I'm sorry things just can't seem to work

And just so you know, I never intended to make you hurt

Or to disrespect you and your self-worth,

But I did,

And no amount of apologies could take that all back

All the selfish things I've done to you in the past

Or all the things I should've done but I always lacked

You deserve someone who can cherish you

Someone you can see a future with and might get married to

Not someone who will let you jump straight into love without a parachute

I am not her; I will never be who you need

This is the best thing for us, even if we don't agree

So, goodbye my love, move on and be free

You will always be my favorite memory.

"Closure."

I called you last night, and I wish I had a better reason

But it's time I stop running and time I start feeling

I'm confused,

It's been days, months, and years since I've felt pain from you

Since I've felt pain, at all

See 'cause, it was right after you, that I needed alcohol

And I don't blame you for my addiction

But ever since you left, nothing's ever been more different

And by different, I mean shattered

The pain you rooted in me caused nothing else to matter

When you told me it was over

It was the last day I was sober

It was the last day I was faithful

And I've never gotten closure

'Cause you chose her

After you told me you wouldn't

So, I carry my bags and unload them even when I know that I shouldn't

But you did that

The trust issues I have, you built that

And it only took you 8 weeks

It's been 4 years now and I still haven't made peace

'Cause looking back at it, when I was with you, I wasn't drinking

My mind was shut off and my heart did all the thinking

And it played me,

Alcohol isn't ruining my life, it is trying to *save* me

From the pain you inflicted

I thought I knew who you were, I thought you were different

I trusted you,

And to me that means more than saying "I love you"

'Cause the doors I spent closing for my heart's preservation

I opened them to you without hesitation

And I didn't mean to trust you, it happened so suddenly

And I didn't mean to love you, it happened so subtly

You made me feel every emotion

Maybe that's why now I feel so very broken

I felt envy, I felt rage

I felt happy and afraid

I felt sad the day you left me,

All alone, I felt betrayed

And now,

I feel nothing unless I pour these shots down

I felt nothing the day you stopped coming around

I feel...

Nothing

Because you hurt me so bad

And I refuse to feel again if it's anything like that

Do you know, you were the last person I was good to?

What did I do to deserve this, how could you?

You lied when I demanded your honesty

You made me feel like there was something wrong with me

You had me so conditioned

So now I ignore my intuition

And I say "you're all the same" 'cause I can't tell no more who's different

Because you were supposed to be

You made me feel loved, your arms were home to me

And now, I'm homeless

I search for love in the streets but I see now it's hopeless

'Cause I will never again allow myself that uncertainty

Of someone saying they love me, then just end up hurting me.

"Her First Love."

It was puppy love

At least that's what they called it

"As quickly as it came it's gone,"

But we never did fall for it

We fell for each other, both so deep and wrapped tightly

And if this *isn't* love, then I'm scared of what it might be

Because I've seen so many people walk in, and then leave

So many hearts shattered and left at the scene

And I know you're afraid he'll break my heart at eighteen

But Mom, please let me marry the man of my dreams

I love him, I swear, I put that on God

And I know you can't resist the man you look up to a lot

He's in my prayers, Mom

I pray that he's strong

I pray for our love and hope nothing goes wrong

I pray for our future, I want a home and six kids

And I've never wanted anything more than I've ever wanted this

Mama, please say you'll say yes

Whether you think you know what's best

Put your fear aside and help me pick out my white dress

Because I am marrying that man, whether or not you are a guest

...

I remember our first kiss, skipping class holding hands

We even played together in our school's marching band

We talked all hours of every waking day

Our love was so strong, **God himself, couldn't take it away**

Communication is key, and we were like janitors

But still they told us our love was too young and amateur

Don't tell me we're too young, that we're dumb and naïve

'Cause I heard my own father scream love then pack his bags up and leave

I've seen marriages fail, I am aware of the statistics

But our love has jumped through hoops and proven its persistence

...

And just as he was ready to give up all the stress

I said "Babe! Guess what…she said yes!"

Shopping frantically for flowers, shoes, and a veil

It's a dream come true, my own personal fairytale

I shed tears of excitement, shed tears of relief

I finally get to marry the man of my dreams.

"I Do."

Wedding bells ringing

Church choir singing

As we step out as "Mr. and Mrs."

Showing our affection with hugs and kisses

My mom shed tears, as she saw me in white

Seeing me the happiest I've been so far in my life

Freshly nineteen, with my heart filled to the rim

So thankful to have met someone like him

Someone who will love me without hesitation

Without any limits, without expiration

We vowed forever, for richer or poor

And to start a family with him, was all I was hoping for

We were young in love, and infatuated

Drunk off love, completely intoxicated

He was my drug, and I was severely addicted

'Cause a life without him was a life I couldn't live in...

Unfortunately, our love story had to be rewritten

Because the ending was something no one could've predicted

He was dying, and I had not the slightest clue

That our only memory as husband and wife was when we said, "I do."

"My Guardian Angel."

They say with time, pain eases

That your heart will learn to love again even in tiny pieces

That no matter how badly this affects you right now

You'll fight this feeling someway, somehow

The cut is still fresh, as you were just put to rest

But the memories they live, I will never forget

The excitement in your eyes as I walked through the door

I didn't know then, what you were so happy for

But ever since you left, no one could ever love me more

On the days I was sick, you were right by my side

You'd run so fast when you heard me cry

But where are you now?

As I drown myself in tears saying goodbye

Goodbye? Did I really just say those words?

To someone I love, nothing can be worse

Than losing the person who meant the universe

You'll never know

How hard it was to let you go

How much it sucked to hear the news

To know there was nothing I can do

Because in a split second, I already lost you

And now I'm lost too

Because now, my days are dreadful long and empty

It's only been a couple, but it feels like a century

I stay up late at night tossing and turning

'Cause I can't stop thinking and my heart won't stop yearning

For the day you burst in and say you're returning

I wasn't ready...you left without warning

You left me without practice on how to mourn and

Now I struggle to lift my head high

Because no amount of "it'll be okays" will ever apply

To the amount of pain I feel inside

Crying...and it won't seem to end

Why did I have to lose my best friend...

I see you in my dreams,

And you smiled as I touched your face

Then you tell me what it's like to be in a "better place"

Because that's what they say right?

 "A better place"

But tell me, how can it be better when between us is so much space

When the only thing I want to feel is your embrace

But from here to heaven there's no staircase

I remember seeing your eyes light up, right before you left me

Then, I remember seeing your eyes dazed out, blank, and empty

Your body was still, but your heart was so strong

The last breath you took was wrapped in my arms

I just wish there was another way you could live on...

When I saw your grave dug, six feet deep

I-

...

I-I nearly choked on my tears and dropped to my feet

Because that's the last sight I wanted to see

...

I couldn't watch when they started to bury him

Because they accidentally threw rocks and I screamed "YOU'RE HURTING HIM!!"

But he wasn't getting hurt, because nothing can hurt him anymore

So, I don't know what I was so upset for

It'll never be the same without him by my side

The hardest thing I had to do was say goodbye

Because I,

Saw his heartbeat go one...two...three...four

One...two...no, more...

In the blink of an eye, and with the touch of a button

He was gone, and I was left with nothing.

SEX.

"Inside."

As a woman, your worth is determined by who's in your bed

And your value decreases the more times you open your legs

And like a 7-11, not a day goes by closed

'Cause they never taught you self-respect it was never shown

So the "know your worth" never works

Like the "love yourself" and "put you first," it's all words

Of a language you can't seem to grasp

'Cause you don't know what it means to take things slow you always moved way too fast

And, you're out of breath

They say a piece of you goes missing every time that you have sex

And you gave out so many pieces that you don't have any left

And now, all you feel is hollow

'Cause they lead you to the bedroom and all you do is follow

Left, right, left, right and sometimes you wish you've forgotten how to walk

They say a woman's body is an elaborate map and sometimes you wish they got lost

In your eyes, not in your thighs

Physical attraction is common in most, but beauty comes from who is inside

So, who's inside?

"Scarlet Letter."

I'm laying down on your side of my bed

Wishing the pillows I cry into were your arms instead

I'm reaching out, eyes shut, with my lips quivering

As I try to hold onto your smell that's still lingering

It smells like arrogance, betrayal, and mostly dishonesty

Like the acceptance of a hurt that never got an apology

You are nonexistent,

Physically you are there, but emotionally you are distant

It sounds too familiar,

Like I've said these words aloud

I can scream DADDY ISSUES all I want, but I am talking to a deaf crowd

Because they listen 'til I'm ready to slip down my pants

'Til I'm vulnerable enough to give them a chance

I fall right into their traps, and play right into their hands

"WYD"

A three-letter text that's got me eager to leave

Eager and willing to spend a night or three

With men I do not know and are not right for me

"YO"

Another text I get sent at night

Followed by "YOU UP?" at 3am or those big emoji eyes

"WASSUP?"

And sometimes I think that I'm asking for too much

But I'm not looking to date I'm just looking to fuck

But I'm not looking for lust, I'm looking for love

Honestly, I can't even tell the difference

I let men like you in, without the fear of commitment

With every ounce of liquor, I find myself drinking

It's easy to mask the pain than ever really admitting,

I'm scared...

What if I find love and I'm not prepared?

Or worse, what if I get hurt? More than I've already been

See, love is too strong of a game and I never seem to win

'Cause after the hangover fades, and I've caught another body

I can never rid the shame that's permanently tattooed on me

Like the Scarlet Letter, everyone sees me and can see that I'm damaged

And nobody wants somebody when everybody's already had it

So, they never call me after sex

And after the third unanswered text,

I get drunk again and I'm onto the next

See after Bryan, there was Reese, Tyrone, Mitch and James

So many guys in my bed, and I don't even know all their names

And I try to flip the script, but the story still remains

They get all the sex, and I get all the pain.

"Guys Like You."

I can't tell if it's guys like you, or girls like me

Who reflect and project their insecurities

Who neglect and accept all the immaturity

To perfect and protect a man you know he could never be

A woman, I can never be

See,

I think it's time that I start to accept

That I'm always the girl you call just to have sex

I'm the girl who never wins, I'm not even second best

I'm the girl who always stays, but always gets left

I am naïve,

I give more love to others than I have ever received

I'm so desperate for compassion because somewhere I believe

That falling in love is a goal I can achieve

But, I guess I gotta accept the fact that, that'll never be me.

"Master of Manipulation."

"Don't piss me off"

I'm sorry, was it something I said

"Don't piss me off you're doing it again"

I'm sorry, getting you mad was never part of my intentions

I didn't even say anything, I ain't even mention the-

You know what, never mind, because you'll always end up right

And I'm not in the mood to lose another fight

'Cause you'll raise your voice, and I'll cower in fear

Trying to dodge the disrespect and cover my tears

'Cause, I can't show you I'm weak, because you love the control

I'm a prisoner for your love and you'll never grant me parole

You feed me words that are backhanded compliments

Like "look who's finally listening and learned some common sense

What do you bring to the table besides your pussy and ass?

You know, I don't like that many people but you're not all that bad"

Hands on my lap, mouth shut, and I'm frozen too

If there's one thing you taught me was to speak when you are spoken to

Yes sir

No sir

Please, and *always* thankful

Incur

Recur

And each time it's more painful

But my feelings stick out, like a big sore thumb

I don't think I'm building a tolerance I think I'm getting more dumb

'Cause I've read books about guys like you

About the different stages and phases of abuse

About the cycle that never ends

And the women who sweep it under the rug and just play pretend

And I was always so angry at the women who remained stagnant

In relationships filled with self-hatred and sadness

And they stay…

I, stay…

And I can't quite put my finger on it, the reason I keep coming

I guess it's better to be treated like shit than to be treated like nothing

I'd rather settle for the yelling, the screaming, the roaring disrespect

The low-quality dead-end meaningless sex

I'd trade it all for healthy but that just makes too much sense

I like the complications

The fights and intimidation

Why else would leaving cause such a hesitation

I need your approval, even if I only get it once weekly

I just have to know that in a world so ugly, there's someone out there that needs me

Because when the dust begins to settle, and the flames die down

You know, you're actually not that bad to be around

But when the fires lit, oh God, it combusts

And I take a step back and I look back at us

And **I AM NOT HAPPY**...

I'm not happy...

But I will deny it to my grave if anyone ever asks me

Because I love the complications

The fights and intimidation

But there's nothing I love more than the master of manipulation

And that's you.

"Fuck Him."

He said he needed time, then outta nowhere he just dipped

No two weeks or nothing, and he ain't even tell you shit

Caught off guard, 'cause you thought things were alright

Now you crying staring at his IG all night

'Cause you catching the subs and passive aggressive posting

Said he likes to keep a private life but he's out here boasting

'Bout his next big moves, 'bout his next big shots

'Bout how he's so proud to be fucking with these thots

He's deliberate

Inconsiderate

You gave him your heart and words can't describe what he did to it

But, all that bad shit fades

And all that pain goes away

When you hear his fucking voice, or see his stupid face

He's got you hypnotized, like you're in some kind of trance

So he manipulates you into thinking that he's worth another chance

But there comes a point in time when you realize what you're worth

So, you leave and don't look back no matter how much it hurts

'Cause it kills you

To know the person who empties your heart was the same who used to fill you

But you keep your "head straight" and take his advice

So, you crying at home but post "I'm living my best life"

Then you see his followers skyrocket and

You finally build the courage to unfollow and block him

Then shorty posts some pics, and he dies of dehydration

But remember y'all broke up, so he owes no explanation

He left you, 'cause he wasn't ready to take the next step

Then you catch his ass on tinder and he ain't swiping to the left

He's got a new girl, he's talking oh so slick too

Thinks he's in love 'cause she puts up with his shit and gave it up quick too

Now she's getting the same treatment you had

Getting fill ins to match his fucking durag

You mad

Mad he wasn't man enough to wanna build and stay

Mad he's giving her the love he should've gave you from the first day

It hurts, don't it?

To be left out of the team and treated like an opponent

To know yesterday he said your name, but now it's her name that he's moaning

It's her name on his phone, and it's her name he stays calling

And it's her bed now he's waking up to every morning

When it should've been you

'Cause it could've been you

You tried everything on Earth so that it would've been you

But would've, could've, should've, doesn't stitch up your cuts

And would've, could've, should've, doesn't fix y'all back up

'Cause now she's got his attention

She's riding with him but ain't got no sense of direction

So y'all can have your matching sets

And y'all can have your trashy sex

Just watch out for him sis, 'cause he'll do you dirty next

'Cause he's a **FUCKBOY**

He walks, talks and traps like one

Claiming he's a real man but never acts like one

And you feel stupid for believing him

Stupid for seeing something he don't even see in him

He used to laugh at you, but guess who's laughing still

It's true, 'when a good woman leaves your life everything goes downhill'

'Cause he got, NO JOB, and NO AMBITION

NO GOALS, JUST HOPEFUL WISHING

And now he wanna text you like everything's just fine

It's like he got an alert on his phone that he finally left your mind

Now you're feeling so torn, like Letoya Luckett

Part of you wants to respond but the other half says fuck it

So you're burning a hole thru your screen just staring at his name

Thinking "how can he be so nonchalant after causing so much pain"

After not giving a fuck,

About leaving so abrupt

He **DOES NOT** have the right to come back once you finally gave up

Once you crossed him out your heart, once you crossed him out your mind

That shit was not easy it took a long time

For you to feel okay, and not that "fake it 'til you make it"

You can bounce back from a scratch, but he took your heart to break it

He took all of your feelings and tried to manipulate it

HE FUCKED YOU RAW SO MANY TIMES THEN CLAIMED Y'ALL NEVER DATED

FUCK HIM.

"After Hours."

You crave me only when light fades to darkness

A crave for love but a love so heartless

With a single text, young and naïve

I'm on the road doing full speed

Racing to your house like the **IDIOT** that I am

Pretending that I could be alright

Going to your house in the middle of the night

When being with you makes the tears harder to fight

But when you ask me "What's wrong?"

I say "I'm just fine."

As if you really care what's on my mind

Quit talking to me, you're just wasting your time

I'm here for business only, aren't I?

This is what I had started originally

Didn't think I'd care at first, but now it's kinda hitting me

Like a shot straight to the chest

And it was clear from the beginning this was all about sex

And believe it was but now I'm trying my best

Trying my best to keep my mouth shut

It's okay to have sex with me every night casually but to be something more I'm not good enough

You can commit to having casual sex

But too afraid to commit and take the next step

Like a cordless phone, no emotional attachments

You and I used to mean something, what the fuck happened?

So, tell me

Why can you get off in treating me the way that you do

And even when I know I deserve someone better I *still* come running back to you

Time and time again, after I just finished hurting

And what kills me the most is you don't have the decency to treat me like a person

After what we just did?

And I can't get a goodnight kiss?

Is there something wrong with my lips?

Because you didn't seem to have a problem when they were all over your dick

And now you throwing me out your house as if I never meant shit

As if you never wanted this

As if I made the whole thing up in my head and this never did exist

BUT NO

But no...

This is what I signed up for, and this is what we agreed to

Too weak to go on without you but I hate admitting that I need you

So, I settled for the casual things and whatever I could to please you

'Cause seeing you every now and then

Was better than never seeing you again

But look at me here, stuck at a dead end

Praying and hoping we could be something more when I can't even call you my friend

I loved you

And you used me

And I just let you

So how can I move on freely when you made it so hard to forget you

And you can't see

How hard it is for me

To go to your house and have sex casually

Knowing that this is all it'll ever be

Knowing that is my worth to you

Knowing that this isn't affecting or hurting you like the way it's killing me

I was stupid to think that "after hours" could ever more to you

But I'm smart enough now to know I'm nothing but a whore to you

But stupid enough still, to open all the doors for you

But now I'm racing off, in the opposite direction

Avoiding confrontation and avoiding rejection

But you run to me and follow me and force to say what's wrong with me and the conversation goes as follows:

"It's best if I don't say it, you don't wanna hear it anyways

You never cared about me before what makes tonight different than the other days"

"You seem stressed just tell me please what's on your mind"

"For the millionth time, I swear to god I'm just fine!!"

Running away again, banging my hands into the steering wheel

That was my golden opportunity to tell you how I feel

Crying all through the night

Crying when I hit the red light

I pick up my phone and I start texting your name

Thinking to myself "you're not worth all this pain"

So the text I sent was something I thought you should know

"I just can't keep doing this anymore" and your response was:

"So don't"

And by that time, it was clear to me

That sex was all this appeared to be

But I just couldn't get up and leave

Because I wanted every part of you

So making the decision to leave was the hardest I had to do

Knowing my worth, and saying it to myself constantly

Another lesson learned, but everyday still haunting me

And I will **NEVER** be that girl you call to have sex with and then just dismiss

It took me way too long to realize, but I know now that I am so much better than this shit.

"Blackout."

You said you didn't mean to...

And that you were caught in a moment

But when I say the word "RAPE," you never seem to own it

I should've known better, because this has happened way before

And every time I think I'm loved I give it my all and more

So, maybe I'm to blame for this, because I read all the warnings

And this isn't the first time I woke up to someone in the morning

I-I know it looks bad...but I swear I didn't want to

Because a decision made in the heat of the moment is the one that always haunts you

I left my house that night...without any intention of having sex

But when liquor gets involved there's no telling what happens next

I don't remember what was said...but I know I made the call

But tell me, how can you get consent from someone who's bumping into walls

Someone with slurred speech, closed eyes, and every five seconds that goes by falls

I woke up naked...physically and emotionally

As you smiled at me...cynically and soullessly

Are you proud of yourself?

Do you feel like 'the man?'

Like you accomplished a goal that was part of your life plan?

Do you feel **WHOLE**?

Like the way I feel *e m p t y*?

You could've chose someone else, *anyone* else, I'm sure consenting women there's plenty

I justified your actions 'cause I didn't think I could be raped

And when I think of that word, I think of held against your will, or being duct taped

I KNEW THAT RED MEANT STOP, AND THAT GREEN MEANT GO

BUT I DIDN'T THINK A DRUNK YES MEANT A SOBER NO

I remember throwing up in my bathroom sink

Because I couldn't hold down any more of my drink

I was incoherent, and unable to consent, wouldn't you think?

Shouldn't you have thought twice before helping me get undressed

Before you put your hands through my hair and kissed down from my neck

Before you-

...I can't remember the rest

I was too drunk to slow down the pace we had fastened

And how can I feel pain from a memory pitch black and,

How can I call this rape, when I'm not even sure it happened

I had to ask you why I was laying down unclothed

You spoke nothing but the truth but I wish lies you told

'Cause now this black memory I am forced to hold

BECAUSE EVERY BIT OF INNOCENCE I HAD LEFT YOU STOLE

So, let me ask you something

Did it ever occur to you to stop…just once?

Please answer the question I've been dying to know, for months

I suppressed this horrific blackened memory

That damaged my mind and put my life in jeopardy

I was two weeks late and thought it could be yours

You said you wore a condom but how do I know that for sure?

How do I know that you took all the necessary precautions

When you did this to me when I was unconscious

I was belligerent and a mess

How could you even enjoy the sex

It's not fair that you get to discard this memory and I can *never* forget

You look me in my eyes, and feel no remorse

You said "we're both grown adults" so that gives you the right to force

Your way through a door I didn't unlock for you

But you were determined to get in and there was no stopping you

You stripped me down and now every day I walk alone and naked

And actively try to restore all the damage that you created

But, I gotta give it to you tho, 'cause it takes someone real brave

To have the audacity to not call what you did rape

Now let me ask you something else, 'cause I just can't seem to let it go

Did you rape me drunk because you knew if I was sober, I'd say no?

Depression.

"First Date Questions."

What if I told you, I wasn't okay?

And the only reason I called was to make the suicidal thoughts go away

What if I said I'm too scared to be alone

And even though it's childish you bring me peace over the phone

What if I sobbed uncontrollably?

Would you hang up immediately or stay on the phone with me

And if I drop the call on purpose, would you keep calling until you get a hold of me

What would you do if I said I couldn't explain how I feel?

Would you tell me it's in my head and that my pain is not real

Or would you hold me when I'm lonely and pray one day my scars will heal

Tell me,

Because this isn't up for debate

My anxiety and my depression will always come on our dates

And I'd rather tell you now before you find out way too late

Before you find me on my bed, just wallowing in my sadness

With the negativity in my head I cling to you just like a magnet

So, with all that being said, is this a life you can imagine

Because you and I, are the kind of opposites that never end up attracting

Is it okay...that I'm not?

I'm just trying to make you comfortable I understand that it's a lot

I understand if you want to bail, you can leave before your entrance

'Cause my mind is like a jail and depression is a life sentence

And there are NO visitors...

Am I making myself clear?

There will be days I want you far but times I need you here

Like when my thoughts take control and I hear these voices in my head

That whisper such sweet nothings like I'm better off just being dead

Cutting deeper in the skin, and closer to the vein

I don't cut because it hurts, I cut to feel the pain

And I don't mean to cut you off, I'm just cutting to the chase

'Cause I like to take things slow, but depression has its own pace

So, these are all the things I struggle with internally

But anyways, my favorite color is burgundy.

"Replaced."

I'm scared...

I'm scared to get too close

I'm scared I'll lose you right when it hurts the most

Right when the weight of the world is sitting on my shoulders

And right when my anxiety is about to topple over

Right when I need you...

It's terrifying to think

As quickly as you entered my life, you're gone in the next blink

The next second, I'm screaming into my trembling palms

Crying...where did this go wrong

I told you I needed your support, and you just laughed in my face

I reached out for your hands and all I got was space

Empty...

When I ask for help and you're not there

Empty...

When I play it off like I don't care

Right when I need you...

But she's all you need

It's okay, I get it, it's a better view from the backseat

I've watched everyone I know walk away with a piece of me

I needed you more than you ever needed me

I need you...

Right now,

Because these nights are dark

Because I'm running out of room on my body to make this bloody art

Because every time something good comes along it always falls apart

And I'm tired of having to glue back these pieces of my heart

I'm sorry I'm flawed, and that you have to reassure me

Every second of everyday because of my high insecurities

But can you blame me?

She's beautiful, outside and in

She's smart, she's funny, she's talented and thin

She's everything I'm not, but she's all I want to be

Because maybe if I'm her, then maybe you'd want me

I'm alone, and I miss the days when you were blind

When I was the only thing that consumed your mind

When I had your devoted undivided attention

When I had your heart without any extension

I need you...

Please tell me you'll be there

Don't tell me you're another thing in my life I have to cut up and share

Because all my life, I've had people take and take and take

And when they look her in her eyes, I get replaced, replaced, replaced

She's my sister,

She's my neighbor,

She's my coworker,

She's my friend,

She's the girl you follow on Instagram, the list just never ends

See, cause, it doesn't matter who she is, it matters who I'm not

And even if I were the last person on Earth, she'd still take my spot.

"Caged Thoughts."

Sometimes, I wish I didn't open my mouth

Sometimes, I wish I didn't open my heart

Sometimes, I wish I didn't open anything

Doors, my ears, my mind

My eyes...

Sometimes I wish I wasn't alive

And by alive I don't mean breathing

When I say "please kill me now" I don't mean in life I mean with these feelings

'Cause depression is insane

Has you seeing the world up in flames

And no amount of antidepressants can help the chemical imbalance in your brain

'Cause it's larger than that

It comes then it goes so it gets harder to track

And when it's here it's bad

I'm talking 'bout withdrawn from all endeavors

With feelings of incompetence that doesn't end ever

That doesn't end well

That doesn't blend well

With the way society thinks I should feel, I'd be damned hell

If they try to cage my feelings like I'm in a damn cell

My mind is an animal, and I am my own prey

And when an animal is hungry nothing can get in its way

And when it's done, depression will still eat at my carcass

Defeated and helpless and into the darkness

I am dead

With a smile on my face that's so hard to pretend

And the weight on my chest it's not hard to resent

The people who carry their lives with content

Is the person I wish I could be once again

Why can't I be like them?

I want to so badly,

I don't want to change who I am

I just want to be happy

I just want to feel alive

I just want to feel inside

I just want to see the world from a different set of eyes

I just want to want to live

I don't want to feel like this

I just want to walk through life one day and know what happy is.

"Homesick."

Depression has a way of making white sand, and clear water

Feel like,

The day we buried my grandfather

Still…

With my feet in the ocean

I'm just going through the motions

Wondering, if this doesn't make me happy, what ever will?

Am I destined to be depressed?

Because lately, it seems like the only thing I do best

Lately it seems like all I ever am is fucking stressed

And lately it seems like the more I get off, the more pressure falls on my chest

I'm uncomfortable

Uneasy

Awkward

And embarrassed

I wonder if they know I feel this way, and that's why they keep staring

I just want to go home

Where the closets aren't filled with last season's depression

Where the mirror projects a more positive reflection

Where my mind and my body create the strongest connection

And the sight of self-love shines through every dimension

I just want to go home

To a place that is free of all negativity

Where the voices stop screaming but sing proudly in symphonies

Where depression no longer keeps me kept in captivity

I just want to go home, to a person I can love

I just wish I were home…

But I never knew exactly where that was.

"Monkey Bars of Hope."

I've been over-thinking

Been in my head so much lately I started over-drinking

I started over-talking, I started over-sharing

I started over-feeling, but never over-caring

Not about myself

Not about the damper I put on my mental health

Not about my wrists and the scars that I've caused

Not about the victories, but every battle I've ever lost

It always comes back to me

And maybe I'd stand a chance fighting if instead it came back gradually

But no matter what I do, this depression stays attacking me

And I just keep losing,

I put my best foot forward like they tell me so I don't know what more I should be doing

Should I, surround myself with people when all I'm feeling is alone

Or should I mask the pain in bottles because that's all I've ever known?

Should I talk about it? Because that helps right?

But we all know a person with depression never does and if they do it's a rare sight

'Cause it's swept under the rug

And no one gives a fuck

Then when you're chained down to a hospital bed, they wanna ask "where is this coming from?"

Everyone is so fucking oblivious

Depression isn't when they run out of your pumpkin spice latte Becky,

It's serious

It's caused me anxiety, and anxiety caused me nightmares

So, I wrestle my mind to sleep and it never seems to fight fair

Sometimes, I break down…I mean, really break down

My moods used to swing but now depressions my playground

And the inner child in me, is on the *monkey bars of hope*

Hanging so tightly so I don't fall in the **unhealthy ways to cope**

And I always thought if I just stood there, I'd never take the loss

See, depression *is* the monkey bars and I've never made it across.

"3:28am."

The truth about depression is

It's unpredictable

Unwarranted

Unpleasant

Unapologetic

It's made me do and say terrible things to myself without ever asking for forgiveness because depression makes you feel

Unworthy

Unwanted

Unloved

It's made me believe that I would be better if I just give up

And by give up, I mean suicide

Let's just cut the bullshit

'Cause you can ask all these "prescreening questions" and I promise I am the full list

"Do you ever have trouble sleeping?

Loss of interest in activities?

Do you struggle getting out of bed just to avoid daily responsibilities?

Do you find yourself feeling empty?

And that your life is losing purpose?"

It's funny they ask these questions when depression has different versions

So, let me tell you how it hits me

Head high walking down the street and it comes out and kicks me

Emotions bleeding out but there's no one here to fix me

Laying helpless on the concrete thinking,

"God, why did they pick me..."

It's cold here...

There's no soul here...

I'm in the deepest cave of my own body and I am *alone* here...

Everything is black and white

And, it doesn't help when people keep on trying to send me light

'Cause the truth about depression, it knows with who to pick its fights

And I've been beaten up repeatedly

And we all know snitches get stitches so I've dealt with it in secrecy

Learned to let it just eat at me

Learned to let it take its course and hope it leaves peacefully

Only,

It never does

And sometimes I think I'm better off just going nuts

Cause,

The truth about depression is

IT FUCKING SUCKS.

"Too Late."

It's a deadly combination mixing alcohol with anger

I look myself in the eyes of a mirror and all I see looking back is a stranger

Who are you?

Because you're not the girl I often pretend to be

You are a girl so sad and depressed, you are not a friend to me

You are a bitch,

Cause you manipulate my mind into cutting up my wrists

Into hating who I am, every curve and every inch

Into drinking all my problems till they're gone or that they're fixed

Into seeking validation from a stranger and his dick

You must really hate me...

And I wish I knew what I did

Because even on my enemies I would never wish them this

This, silent cry that breaks every bone in your body down

The feeling of holding it all in so you can let it all out

When you're on the floor of your room, hoping someone hears the music

Or hears the faint screams for help right before you fucking lose it

With the scissors to your wrist ready to abuse it

You hope someone barges in, but they never fucking do it

They never fucking do it...

To Everyone I've Ever Loved,

Inhale... exhale
Everybody makes it look so simple
It's like I remember to breathe in then get lost somewhere in the middle
I forget where I am and lose control of my surroundings
I'm in a pool of my emotions and I can't stop from drowning
I can't stop and rationalize to find a rhyme or reason
I can't remember the last day I had my time or freedom
I can't remember the last day I took a deep sigh
I can't remember the last day I spent without tears in my eyes
I don't know what it feels like to be "normal"
To not have to battle between thoughts of suicide and morals
To not be labeled as too sensitive or overly dramatic
My feelings are what I said, MINE so don't call me problematic
Until you know what it feels like to be underwater breathing
Till you know what it feels like to be wide awake and sleeping
Till you know that breath of relief when you see yourself and you're bleeding
And you've let out all your tears but your insides are screaming
For help
Help me...

It's been a struggle for quite some time
Having to fight off the demons that consume my mind
They've abused me, they've out done me
They've consumed me, they've become me
I smile so wide to cover up all my scars
And by all means I know that my life isn't hard
But what's hard is this pressure
Of having to have it all together
When you're screaming out for help and all they say
is "feel better"
It's easy to be misunderstood
When outside looking in all you see is the good
You can't see it, or grab it
But I feel it, I have it
I look in the mirror and I don't recognize myself
I have this look of evil that calls for supervisor help
And it's scary,
So scary...
To have everyone around you and all you think of
is what they'll say when you're buried
You see nothing but darkness and you're so close
to the end
God wrote out my invite and I'm just waiting
for it to send
Please send
Just take me by car, bus, or plane
I just need to see that "better place" cause
I can't take anymore pain
To everyone I've ever loved, please understand I
feel alone
And nothing will make me happy till I see my name
Carved in stone

As I lay on my bed, throwing used tissues in the trash
I try to think of things that used to make me laugh
And it's not working
God, why isn't it working
It's not fair to feel the pain of a thousand people hurting
To not tell a soul because you don't want them burdened
I've been so strong before but I am such a weak person
I pretend and joke and kid, like everything's just dandy
Cause my feelings are too raw for anyone to understand me
So I broke ties and burnt bridges
Told lies and made decisions
And I've decided . . .
Today's the day ~~I kill myself~~ **I stay alive.**

Love always,
Jess

"It's Never Too Late."

It's hard for her to feel any different

Everyone showers her in compliments, but she doesn't have their vision

She wants to love herself, it's all she ever wishes

But she finds comfort in her pain and every poem she's ever written

She's gifted

It's too bad she can't agree

She beats herself up daily going through all the extremes

And you can tell her that she's worth it, but it's something she won't believe

'Cause it's the most beautiful people who have the lowest self-esteem

And wow, is she beautiful

She's got this burning passion inside her that shines clear right through her eyes

And this crooked gapped tooth smile that she tries so hard to hide

And this laugh, she's got this laugh that she hates but is so rich in its quality

And she knows she loves herself somewhere deep inside subconsciously

She's just broken from her past, and she's just trying to make it through it

She's fighting to love herself, but depression just beats her to it

She's just looking for a reason not to break one day and lose it

And finally see her beauty the way everyone around her views it

She can do it, she's a fighter

I've seen her fight far worse than this

But to love yourself is a job and I don't think you know how hard it is

It's every day, overtime even when you're tired

The kind of job where you can't quit or ever end up fired

It's demanding, and exhausting being the only one of the sidelines

They say you should love yourself but never gave her any guidelines

SHE IS TRYING...

In the best way she knows how

It's never too late to love yourself because she is starting to right now.

Danielle,

Thank you so much for supporting and purchasing my first poetry book, it means so much to me. Allow these words to resonate with you and may you always walk in your purpose. Happy Reading!!

      Love always,
      Jess ♡